The Thirteenth Lake

The Thirteenth Lake

Poems by

Vida Chu

© 2019 Vida Chu. All rights reserved.
This material may not be reproduced in any form, published,
reprinted, recorded, performed, broadcast,
rewritten or redistributed without
the explicit permission of Vida Chu.
All such actions are strictly prohibited by law.

Cover design by Shay Culligan
Cover photograph "The Thirteenth Lake in the Adirondacks"
by Vida Chu

ISBN: 978-1-950462-31-5

Kelsay Books Inc.

kelsaybooks.com

502 S 1040 E, A119
American Fork, Utah 84003

*To my beloved grandchildren
Andrew, Margaret, Colin, and Camille*

Acknowledgments

The author wishes to thank the following journals in which these poems originally appeared, some in a slightly different form.

Kelsey Review: "Dust," "Homecoming," "My Mother's Hands," "The Thirteenth Lake," "Unexpected Correspondence"

The Literary Review: "Sky Burial"

The Patterson Review: "All in the Genes," "China Has 34 Million Single Men"

U.S. 1 Newspaper: "Going Back for the Terra Cotta Warrior," "I Want to Borrow Icarus' Wings," "Stealing Caution," "The Language of Signs"

U.S. 1 Worksheets: "Chinese Grannies Found Their Grooves," "Echoes on the Cliffs," "Everyone Deserves a Happy Ending," "HB#2"

Contents

Prologue
The Thirteenth Lake

Part I The Darkness Fighters

The Historian's Promise to His Dying Father	18
Echoes on the Cliffs	19
Homecoming	20
The Language of Signs	21
Gifts Flung to Heaven Crash Down	22
China Has 34 Million Single Men	23
Chinese Grannies Find Their Groove	24
Three Tales of Jia Yu Guan	25
The Temple Dancer	26

Part II Buddha Rides the Tide

Do You Like Eggs Benedict?	30
Ginkgo in a Foreign Land	31
Ecstatic Dancing, Union Square, NYC	32
The Reconstruction of Adam	33
Just Another October Day in Princeton	34
Turkish Delight	35
The Baksheesh	36
The Dog, the Donkey and the Flimflam Man	37
The Market at Myanmar's Inle Lake	38
Never Tie Balloons on an Elephant's Tail	39
The Alaska Tundra	40
Ahab's Last Thoughts	41
The Retirement of St. Genevieve	42
Envoys of Ra	43
You Can Have Your Cake and Eat It Too	44
Everyone Deserves a Happy Ending	45
Dialogue on the Creation of Insects	46

Part III A Brush Stroke Can Change Everything

Progressive Music to Untrained Ears	50
Sounds of Bali's Gamelans	51
Seeing with Ears	52
Secret of the Master Calligrapher	53
HB #2	54
Movies	55
Knit One, Purl Two	56
My Mother's Hands	57
Dust	58
Sky Burial	59

Part IV All in the Genes

Going Back for the Terra Cotta Warrior	64
Grandma Duty	65
Stealing Caution	66
Grandson in New York City	67
End-of-Life Matters	68
Snakes and Ladders	69

Part V Unexpected Correspondence

I Want to Borrow Icarus's Wings	74
An Unexpected Guest	75
My Silence in the Hospital Room	77
Leaving the Adirondacks	78
The Hotel with the Two-Lane Pool	79
Convex/Concave	80
Untethered	81
The Snake in the Wine Cup	82
Wanderlust	83
The New House	84
Morning Ritual	85

About the Author

Prologue

The Thirteenth Lake

The Thirteenth Lake

The sun dominates the sky. No
clouds dare appear. The air holds
its breath. My footsteps in pine needles,
mosquitoes at my face.
The trail turns into a granite staircase.
The knapsack weighs heavy on my back
and sweat trickles down.

Orange salamanders sun
on moss-covered rocks,
while white birches listen
to the spluttering brook.
A spotted frog leaps out.

I cross ribbons of water, jump splashy puddles—
overspills from beavers' lodges.
Suddenly, a sun-drenched clearing
and my eyes embrace the Thirteenth Lake.

Water mirrors the bare, rocky summit,
slivers of minnows, shadow and light.
On the far shore among reeds,
an empty rowboat waits.

Part I

The Darkness Fighters

The Darkness Fighters

Blind elders in Hong Kong break
the housebound tradition
refuse to live out their lives
in lonely isolation.

They venture to learn
Kung Fu exercise
play two-string erhu by ear
create a sightless rowing team
join the annual dragon boat race.

Unfazed that they cannot see
the logo on their shirts
the dragonhead on the prow
the faces of their fellow participants
they clutch their oars and wait.

Once the air horn blasts
they shout, *Tiu jin bat ho nang!*
Challenge the impossible!
paddle in a hypnotic unity
adhering to the drumbeats.

Energized by cheers of the crowd
cooled by the spray of seawater
they focus on beating all odds
winning the race.

The Historian's Promise to His Dying Father

Choking with tears, Sima Qian knelt
by the deathbed of his father
and promised to finish writing
the history that his father started.

As Grand Astrologer in Han Court, Sima advised emperors
on auspicious days to perform royal ceremonies—
prayers and sacrifices for good harvest on summer solstice
and in his private hours wrote the chronicles of China.

When General Li surrendered to the enemy,
the emperor executed his entire clan. Sima spoke out.
The emperor asked Sima to choose death or castration.
He opted to live so he could finish writing his book.

Although Sima had no sons to carry the family name,
his work made him, The Father of Chinese History.
Though peaches and plum do not speak
Yet people tread a path beneath.

Echoes on the Cliffs

In the late Ming dynasty
after years of wars and natural disasters
the Bo people dreamt of peace.

They dressed their dead in silk
wrapped in bamboo mats,
together with two blue and white porcelain bowls,
one big and one small iron knife,
placed in coffins made from a single log
to hang high above the Yangtze River.

For hundreds of years their bodies rested on the precipice
close to the heavens in the midst of mountains and rivers.
Their coffins, faint echoes on limestone cliffs.

Homecoming

July in Hong Kong, stormy weather.
Every day ninety degrees, steamy like a sauna.
I sweat inside rain gear.
Acquaintances gone vacationing,
relatives long deceased.

Gold jewelry and Chinese medicine shops
pop up at every corner.
Loud Mainlanders roll new suitcases
crowd the streets. Only the old bakery
and the Cantonese-speaking school children
assure me I am back in my childhood home.

The stormy weather encourages
no tram ride to Victoria peak,
no hike on Dragon Back trail,
no swimming at golden beaches,
no bargaining in night markets and Ladies' streets,
and no visits to Wong Tai Sin Temple and the Big Buddha.

I spend a day in the New Territories' Heritage Museum
among dioramas of traditional villages,
urban New Towns, Cantonese Opera Halls,
Chinese brush paintings and calligraphies,
an unexpected exhibition of Bruce Lee.

Who would have guessed this famous Kung Fu Master
was a Philosophy major, wore contact lenses
for public appearances and film shoots,
and loved to cha cha?

On the ninth day as I am heading for the airport,
the sun breaks out.
The skyline of Hong Kong beckons.

The Language of Signs

Colorful, comical talking signs dot American highways.
Governor Cuomo erected hundreds saying *I love NY.*
My favorite is the two 3-D black-and-white cows billboard,
one sits on the back of the other, painting *Eat Mor Chikin.*

Billboards in China are political propaganda
on Chinese Spirit, Image, Culture, and Voices.
They overshadow street names.
When one asks for direction, he is often told:
Turn left at the big electronic screen of President Xi,
cross the bridge flying the anti-corruption banner,
walk toward the wall poster of happy dancing children
and the store will be on the right.

Foreigners who don't know the language are often lost.
Once in Germany my husband parked a rental car on a street.
I painstakingly copied down the exact street name sign
only to discover later the words said, "One Way Street."

Gifts Flung to Heaven Crash Down

An old banyan tree in Lam Tsuen, Hong Kong
is rumored to be imbued with lucky power.
People come to light incense and lob wishes
tie onto oranges over its branches.
They are convinced their requests will come true,
once the fruits dangle on the bough.

During New Year, thousands come to toss wishes.
On the fourth day, an overburdened tree limb snaps.
It scratches the head of a four-year-old boy
and breaks the leg of an old man.
People stare at the lucky tree
as gifts flung to heaven come crashing down.

China Has 34 Million Single Men

No more arranged marriages.
No nuptial want ads on trees or lampposts.
Today, marriages are dictated by women
who pick and choose their men.

A bachelor over twenty-six is desperate.
He learns peacocking from Dating 101—
how to cut and style his hair, how to dress
in a narrow-collared shirt and fitted pants.

Online@WeChat
He sips tea and nibbles dim sum
with a forlorn, pensive look,
A Brief History of Time by his side.

Silently he bargains with Buddha,
promising to light incense,
if some woman will deliver him
from his lonely bed.

Chinese Grannies Find Their Groove

Legions of women, obliged to retire in their fifties,
dutifully serve family dinner each dusk before
dashing off to parks and public plazas to shuffle
and sashay under bright lights to blaring pop tunes.

The louder the music, the more the fun, they say.
Much better than sitting at home and watching TV.

Neighbors irate at the din, throw rocks, spray water,
fire air rifles and set their dogs on them.
Yet the throbbing disco music continues
as the unperturbed grannies shimmy on.

Three Tales of Jia Yu Guan

> Jia Yu Guan, the westernmost outpost of China's Great Wall, faces
> the Gobi Desert and is the gateway to the ancient Silk Road.

Most ancient travelers were of ambivalent minds about
leaving the fortress for the vast mysterious desert.
They foretold their fortune by throwing stones at the Wall.
If the stones bounced back, they would safely return.
If not, their journey was doomed.

Officials out-of-favor with the emperor were banished
through the West Gate. Mindful that they could never return
and must leave everything behind, they inked
frantic messages and poems on archway walls, begging
heaven for mercy, before stepping into the vast unknown.

Legend claims when the architect requested 99,999 bricks
to build the fortress, he was jeered for his low estimation.
The draftsman obliged by adding one more to the list. In 1372
when Jia Yu Guan Fort was completed, one brick was left,
and to this day, it sits on top of the East Gate—*The Last Brick.*

The Temple Dancer

With a crown of white jasmine
on her jet-black hair,
apricot silk blouse
and gold trimmed emerald green sari,
the dancer waits
motionless as a statue.

At the sound of gongs and flutes
her arms and hands slither like snakes.
Silver ankle-bells jingle at each stamp of her foot.
She twirls, hops and quiver like an aspen leaf.

With palms pressed
her neck darts from side to side.
The face and hand-gestures express joy or sorrow.
But it is her eyes that said it all—
quick, swift glances for fear
or half-closed for passion.

The dance brings ancient mythology to life—
she, the go-between of heaven and earth.

Part II

Buddha Rides the Tide

Buddha Rides the Tide

Anchored in a cove off East River
an inflatable Buddha ten feet tall
sits on a wooden lily pad.

Dog walkers, tourists and passers-by wonder
how long before a flying twig or rock
would puncture this statue full of air.

He bobs back and forth with the tide
allowing Manhattan's city bustle
to filter through his transparent skin.

Do You Like Eggs Benedict?

True love stories are boring
as hard-boiled eggs.
Wouldn't you like to try
a little Hollandaise sauce?
Perhaps a tale about
the hankering of a married man,
like a Buddhist monk's craving
for a crispy roast duck.

See the frozen sunny-side-up smiles
in the Style section
of the Sunday paper.
These couples are dreaming of
perfect omelets that cannot
be scrambled or poached.

Ginkgo in a Foreign Land

I stand tall in temple gardens,
my leaves fan-shaped and green.
My ancestors lived among dinosaurs.
I am a living fossil, a botanical oddity,
the platypus of the plant kingdom.

In the West we are city trees,
we resist air pollution, pests and diseases.
Our leaves lengthen memories.
Our pungent seeds are a Chinese delicacy.

In autumn when days grow short
Maples blaze with crimson fires,
their leaves fall free one-by-one.
But when my green leaves change to saffron,
they drop as if synchronized
blanketing the ground in gold.

Ecstatic Dancing, Union Square, NYC

Check your mind at the door and shimmy in.
No shoes, drugs, or alcohol.
No phones, no cameras, no talking on the dance floor.

Flap like a flag on a breezy day.
Hoot, whoop, chirp, or squawk,
twist and sway, pliable as a rag doll.

Let the world whirl you into a trance.
Lose your stiffness in the dance hall,
then float softly out the exit door.

The Reconstruction of Adam

When Adam fell
his head was severed, his body broken into 28 pieces.

Scientists and engineers
at the Metropolitan Museum of Art
labored for over twelve years
using images from CT scans
to work on his head, hands, knees and feet.
They inserted fiberglass pins in his ankles and wrists
filled cracks and holes with matching color
adhered all body parts and reattached
his head with a new nose.

The resurrected Adam stood
six-foot-three in the courtyard.
The polished marble torso leaned
against the serpent-entwined tree trunk,
eyes fixed on the fragrant luscious fruit
between fingers in his raised left hand
dallying, *Should I serve God or Eve?*

Just Another October Day in Princeton

Forty-two-hundred people went through security.
By eight-thirty, they sat in Jadwin Gym
watched as photographers knelt five rows deep
between the aisles with cameras aiming
at the colorful, silk-hanging sacred tanka.

At nine-thirty all rose on their feet
as a smiling monk in orange robe sauntered in
flanked by Dean Boden and an interpreter.
The 14th Dalai Lama gestured the audience to sit
then donned the orange Princeton baseball cap.

Brothers and sisters! People ask me why
I have not visited Princeton before.
Not possible, I said, because I was never invited.
My biggest regret is I didn't take my studies more seriously.
I learned compassion as a child from my mother.
She let me ride on her back and steer by pulling on her ears.

Before leaving Princeton, His Holiness blessed the mandala
that the monks had been working on the entire day
depicting the paradise of the Buddha of Compassion.
Silently he watched them sweep the sand into a ceramic vessel,
walk down Washington Road,
and pour the content into Carnegie Lake.

Turkish Delight

For twenty dollars the attendant hands me
a pair of plastic slippers,
one folded towel,
and a disc stamped *massage.*

Disrobed, I enter an atrium
where bodies are scattered
like prostrated disciples.
Lie down, a voice commands.

I recline on the heated marble platform
and gaze at eternity through the crystal dome.
Minutes trickle by in beads of perspiration.
Under the glass paneled ceiling
a naked bulb dangles
like a soul in purgatory.

Finally, she arrives, the very image
of Mother Goddess Catal Hoyuk
with bulging stomach and sagging breasts.
She ladles me with warm water,
scrubs and drizzles oily soap
down my skin.

Her palms speedily press my back,
fists hammer my shoulders,
fingers squeeze my neck.
Good? she asks.
G-o-o-d! I moan.

She pulls me to the fountain steps
and baptizes me with water
until I splutter and cannot breathe.
Finished, she says and shoos me out.

The Baksheesh

Bring at least forty singles, the guide advises.
Most souvenirs in Egypt cost a dollar.
As the bus bounces toward the Valley of the Kings
I check my bag for camera, water bottle,
and ten stapled-together dollar bills.

At the gate, a native in his galapiyeh[2] tears my ticket.
A rifle-swinging policeman steps forward
plunges his hand into my belongings,
fishes out the camera, turns it this way and that
and waves me on with the flick of his hand.

Venders converge like vultures,
pushing beads, headscarves and antiquities.
I reach for a dollar to pay for an accordion of postcards
and discover that my money has vanished—
the policeman's baksheesh[1].

[1]baksheesh- a tip for service
[2]galapiyeh- a loose Egyptian gown for men

The Dog, the Donkey and the Flimflam Man

Somewhere along the Ring of Kerry's 109-mile drive,
our bus took a photo-stop. Not for the cows and sheep
clotting the lush, rolling Irish hills, but for a wayside vendor.
He sat ruddy-faced on a plastic chair
folding rushes into St. Brigid's Cross. Beside him,
a yellow dog stood on the back of a dark brown donkey.

We bought his cross at two euros a piece,
snapped pictures of the obedient beasts
that stood so still as if hypnotized.
As the bus pulled away, the driver asked,
What do you think he is really selling?
The whole bus chorused, *St. Brigid's Cross.*

He laughed and shook his head.
Those who know travel miles for his poteen.
If you lay twelve euros in his hand, he'll disappear
into the tall grass and fetch you
a three-quarter bottleful of home-made whiskey.

The Cross of St. Brigid is just a myth.
It's the drinks that sustain our Irish spirit.

The Market at Myanmar's Inle Lake

At dawn once every fifth day the Pa'O people come
to barter home-grown chilies, onions and lemon grass
for scissors, mirrors, batteries and plastic bowls.

By mid-morning, tourists land in longboats
armed with cameras, dark glasses, and money belts
to hunt for bargains and treasures among stone necklaces,
carved elephants, brass opium weights, and temple bells.

You say how much, I no angry. Dollars or kyats?
Lucky money, lucky for you, lucky for me.

Behind baskets of corn and tomatoes
women in black gowns with bright headdresses squat
like pigeons, puffing their cheroots, and watch
as foreigners depart for their five-course lunch.

Vendors swarm in, thrusting souvenirs at half-price.
Just look, no problem, very cheap.
While monks returning from their alms rounds
walk in silence, holding their half-filled bowls.

Never Tie Balloons on an Elephant's Tail

A couple wed in Thailand
took an elephant ride to their honeymoon lodge.
Friends tied good-wish balloons to the animal's tail.

The agitated elephant took off.
The mahout gave chase. Underbrush burst the balloons.
The terrified beast charged into the forest.

Battered by tree limbs, the bride screamed and crawled
under the seat. The groom leaped and swung on a bough.
The mahout sweet-talked the passengers to remount

while he jogged beside the lumbering beast.
The newlyweds swayed in their rickety seats
and photographed each other in the changing landscape.

The sky turned crimson when they reached the lodge.
The couple dismounted and toasted each other on the veranda.
The elephant wrapped its trunk around a column and yanked.

Down came the porch and down came the pair.
The wailing bride demanded an annulment.
A fallen flowerpot crowned the groom's head.

The elephant strolled off looking for bananas.

The Alaska Tundra

From June to August in Denali
the season of life erupts.

Fireweeds and bearberry
crimson the tapestry of lichens.

Under the unsleeping sun
angry mosquitoes whine.

Caribou cast their long shadows.
Grizzlies wander with their young.

Tourists arrive in busloads.
Innkeepers hike their prices.

In this brief hundred days
each species finds its niche.

Ahab's Last Thoughts

I shall return
    and be made flesh again
with my ivory leg
    and wait
until you, Moby Dick,
    are beached on shore.

Then I shall slit you
    mouth to anus
peel your blubber
    strip by strip
cut a door in your gut
    haul out your intestines.

And I shall crawl in between the ribs
    and tear
        your heart
            out.

The Retirement of St. Genevieve

You stand on a pedestal in the Luxembourg Gardens
clad in a flowing robe, a shawl on your head,
long braids dangle to your knees.

You, the Patron Saint of Paris,
who witnessed The Revolution,
the guillotining of Louis XVI and Marie Antoinette,
the rise and fall of Napoleon,
two World Wars and the Nazi occupation,
now serenely watch over
sunbathers picnicking on the grass
and listen to the shouts of children
sailing toy boats in the octagonal basin.

You gaze at the distant Eiffel Tower,
unfazed by the few blades of grass
growing from cracks on top of your head.

Envoys of Ra

Who would have guessed
that these grey, fluffy tennis-ball-sized chicks
will grow four feet tall, with slim lengthy legs,
long necks, stunning pink feathers, and a six-foot wingspan.

That they live in colonies numbering tens of thousands
in the highest, buggiest and saltiest lakes
in Africa, Asia, Europe and the Americas.

That they honk like geese,
stand on one leg in the water for hours,
and fly four hundred miles from a running start.

That they synchronize their courtship dance
like Rockettes in Radio City Music Hall,
with head flag, wing salute, and wing-leg stretch.

That they are monogamous, copulate in water
and choreograph their breeding,
so all chicks are born at the same time.

That early Romans ate their tongues as a delicacy.
The Queen of Hearts used them as mallets for croquet games.
We Americans adorn our lawns with their pink plastic forms.

That ancient Egyptians regarded them as envoys of Ra.

You Can Have Your Cake and Eat It Too

Sex was once a terminal experience for the male spider.
As soon as the act was over, the female gobbled him up—
head, body, and all eight limbs.

With a long, slow Darwinian struggle,
male Nursery-Web-Spiders learned
to tie up the female with spider silk

and take off after copulation,
leaving the lady spider to untangle herself
from her sticky, bridal veil.

Everyone Deserves a Happy Ending

For years Conch and Nautilus
on opposite shelves, in a boardwalk store
gathered dust and dreamed of the sea.

I love your iridescent spirals,
Conch whispered.
Wish we'd met in the ocean long ago.

> *And I yearn to be near you*
> *to trumpet your shell*
> *and listen to the waves inside.*

Then one moonless night a hurricane strikes.
Wind rips roofs and flattens walls.
Downpour floods houses and stores.

Conch glides to Nautilus' side,
gathers her up
and they tumble jointly onto the beach.

Rough surf flings them into the water.
Clinging, they waltz out to sea
then softly pirouette down to bed.

Dialogue on the Creation of Insects

for Daniel Chu

The grasshopper is not one of your best creations
Even Aesop made fun of it in 600 BC
On a good day grasshoppers eat grass
but when the fields become parched
they transform into locusts
devouring vegetation in swarms

> *But look at my beautiful and elegant dragonflies*
> *aerialists with iridescent wings*
> *they hover, dive, fly forward, backward*
> *and upside down at 30 miles per hour*
> *They even mate in midair*
> *Their multifaceted eyes can see 360 degrees*
> *Military scientists want to learn*
> *the secret of their precision hunting*

Except you grant them such short existences
after spending four years underwater as nymphs
they have just two months as dragonflies

> *But I gave them a focused life*
> *Made them the prototype*
> *I perfected in my angels*

Part III

A Brush Stroke Can Change Everything

A Brush Stroke Can Change Everything

In ancient China, the artist Zhang was asked
to decorate the monastery's wall.
He painted four realistic dragons
but left their eyes blank.

When bystanders questioned,
Zhang said, *If I had painted the eyes in,*
all four dragons would fly.
The spectators demanded a demonstration.

Zhang dipped his brush into the inkwell,
and dotted the eyes of two dragons.
The sky darkened, lightning flared, thunder growled,
and the pair shot up to the sky.

Progressive Music to Untrained Ears

On a crisp, autumn colored afternoon
innovative music by PUBLIQuartet
evoked images in Wolfensohn Hall.

It opened with the squeaking of an oscillating
rusted-gate, crescendo to spotlight
a dangling body on a lamppost.
The howling of a lone wolf,
a scream from a second-floor window,
and then abrupt silence.

The second movement brought to mind
the sounding of a distant foghorn
echoed by buzzing of mosquitoes,
and belching of bullfrog-courtship calls.

The last movement summoned
the spluttering of a motorboat,
accompanied by squawking ducks
and creaking of the rusted gate.
An unexpected melodious phrase
conjured sunrise mirrored in the lake.

The musicians bowed, the audience clapped,
and during intermission, half left.

Sounds of Bali's Gamelans

People stream into the auditorium
jostling for front-row seats. They eye
the bare-footed, cross-legged musicians
yellow flowers behind their ears
horn-shaped hammers in their hands.

A smack on the *kendhang* drum sets off
at break-neck speed, thunderous clanging
of cymbals, gongs and gamelans
forcing hands on ears
emptying front row seats.

A young boy yells, *It's the ice cream truck from hell!*

Seeing with Ears

Jing-Jing Luo composes music as calligraphy,
different musical instruments for different brush strokes:
woodwind and brass, the starts and jolts
plucked piano strings, the inkblots
violin bowing, the ethereal lines
and silence, the stops and white spaces.

Musical intonations conjure:
the pressing, lifting and meandering
of an ink-laden bamboo brush
languid and dynamic like tai-chi
inking cursive writings onto a horizontal scroll.

Secret of the Master Calligrapher

A friend invited Wang Xizhi for tea
when he failed to show, the friend found him
waddling behind a gaggle of geese.

Wang said, *Observe their elegant and graceful postures,*
the supple strength they push and pull their agile necks.
They teach me to manipulate my brush and use my wrist.

Later Wang became the sage of Chinese calligraphy.
The Emperor admired his writing and was buried with it.
Many people imitated his lettering but few knew
Wang learned from nature in his Daoist belief.

HB #2

for Camille

I have never owned a Mont Blanc.
My son writes exclusively with a fountain pen.
My eye doctor favors a Pentel RSVP fine, purple.
I use the ballpoints given out by banks.

In a drawing class I learn to use a pencil.
This humble writing instrument teaches me
that what is important is not
the outer casing but the inside lead,
that most mistakes can be erased and corrected,
that life, like a pencil, needs constant sharpening,
and with a little shading,
a circle can be turned into a sphere.

Movies

Remember, Mother, how we used to sit
five in a row at the movies,
I between sisters, and you next to Dad
and how you spent the whole time translating
the English dialogue to Cantonese
while we children played telephone
passing your words down the line.

Remember when I was in high school
you fought with Dad and moved out.
We met discreetly in matinees
and whispered in the dark.
I complained the house was too empty.
You said you missed me everyday.
The soundtrack drowned our sobbing.
We walked out with puffy eyes.

Now housebound like an indoor cat
you measure your day from meal to meal.
My daughter asks you to the movies.
You worry about sitting too long in the dark.
Got to do it now, your granddaughter said.
Soon Grandma will no longer remember.

Knit One, Purl Two

Knitting was a fad in the fifties
for Hong Kong housewives.
I dreaded those itchy home-weaved
vests, mittens, and hats that Mother
created while riding on buses, and ferries.

When we came to America in the sixties
people jeered, *Only the institutionalized*
would click clack needles all day long.
Overnight, Mother's hands became idle,
her yarns and needles disappeared with the trash.

Last week *The New York Times* claimed
There are health-benefits in knitting.
Public libraries have organized "knitting circles."
On this wintry day I thought of Mother
and the lavender scarf she was making me when she quit.

My Mother's Hands

Her red lacquered nails
danced across the keyboard.
Fingers adorned with sapphires and diamonds
pulled my hair into braids.
We sisters rushed home after school
for Mama's homemade mango ice cream.
One day she put a match to her old letters,
lifted her suitcases and slammed the door.

Now the nails are cut short,
the knobby arthritic fingers bare.
One age-spotted hand twists
the leash of her faithful Welsh Corgi
while the other gropes the empty mailbox.

Dust

Coarse, uneven grained and chalky grey
scooped from the ceramic jar
scattered by his daughters' hands
under the azaleas
watered with a garden hose
patted down into the earth.

All traces of his ninety-four years
vanished.

Sky Burial

To a Tibetan
once death occurs
the body deserves no solitude
the spine is broken in two
the head placed between the knees
and bound with a white cloth.

On the designated day
ragyapas carry the dead to the mountain top
there sandalwood is burnt to summon the ja-gors,[1]
the cloth unwound
the flesh stripped with large knives
the bones ground and kneaded with barley.

Ostrich-like vultures sweep down in hundreds
consume everything in half an hour,
over-stuffed the birds waddle among rocks
while the bodiless soul
soars
free to reincarnate.

---

[1] Ja-gors are a peculiar species, smaller and uglier versions of an ostrich.

Part IV

All in the Genes

All in the Genes

The kids grow big and I grow old.

#1 Grandson is thirteen.
Says all his friends have cell phones,
promises to use it only in emergency.
After scoring 740 on his SAT, he got his wish
and uses the phone to play games and text to Japan.
Next he announces he wants to drive the car.

#2 Grandson is a fearless and inquisitive nine.
I spy him standing on tiptoe by the gas stove.
Don't touch anything, I scream.
Immediately he turns all six burners on, full blast.
You could have burned down the house!
He looks me in the eye and asks, "How long would it take?"

#3 is truly grand. She is seven, does back handsprings,
plays the harp and sings. But what she loves best is
to compete with her brothers in anything.
She claims she is smart because her mother is smart.
Her mother is smart because her grandmother is smart.
But, grandmother is messy, that's why she is messy.

Even the youngest beats me in breaststroke
but I can still teach them piano.

Going Back for the Terra Cotta Warrior

for Maggie

The bright sun on this cool weekend morning
enticed me to the Elks' flea market in Blawenburg.
I strolled along tables of knickknacks, cookware,
and tools, listened to the friendly banter
among vendors, and picked up a copy of
"The Catcher in the Rye" for fifty cents.

At the last stall, amid turquoise bowls and lime green vases,
I spied a charcoal-gray terra cotta warrior nine-inches tall,
with hair knots, trimmed moustache, breast armor,
and right hand clasped over left.
Three dollars, the woman said and I was tempted
to add this treasure to my cluttered house.

On the drive home I thought of Maggie, the granddaughter
who visited the Age of Empires with me at the Met.
Surely Maggie would like this character.
I turned the car around, race-walked to the last stall,
and willed the statue to be there. But it wasn't.

Refusing to accept my loss, I scanned bowls, pots and pans,
spotted an oblong box labeled *General* with a five dollar tag.
Inside, the terracotta warrior winked at me. I scooped up
my prize, handed five bills to the lady and walked away.
Wait, shouted her husband, *I am glad you returned.*
Here! He handed me two dollars back.

Grandma Duty

for Andrew, Colin and Camille

Driving white-knuckled at 70 mph on Interstate 280
I watch cars zoom past left and right.
See that black Mercedes with the CHEN license plate?
says #1 Grandson. *That's my friend's mother's car.*
Pass him, pass him, shouts Grandson #2.
Yeah and the school bus too! choruses Granddaughter #3.

Guys, this CR-V is ten years old.
If I drive any faster, the engine will fall out.
A sudden quiet
Are they sulking or falling asleep?

Stop the car! shrieks #3. *I am getting carsick.*
From the rear view mirror I spy
#1 playing a game on his computer
while #2 and #3 strapped in car seats on either side
strain to see the screen.
Put it away, I say. *Do you want your sister*
to vomit all over your Mac?

A giant trailer-truck veers into my lane.
I honk, slow, and almost get rear-ended.
Can't you drive a little faster? says #2
I need to go pee.

Stealing Caution

for Colin

Our sidewalk buckled from age and weathering,
hazardous for dog walkers on moonless nights.
The city dispatched a backhoe and crew
to hoist away uneven stones,
layer crushed rocks on loose dirt,
and pour on the cement,
safeguarding their work with
yellow ribbons and orange cones.

My seven-year-old grandson asked
for caution-tape as a birthday present.
Said life was tough to room with a big brother
who regularly tossed his stuff.
And if only he could encircle
all his belongings with yellow tape.

That night under the sliver moon
a woman holding scissors and dressed in black
sidled to the new sidewalk.
Next morning when the sun peeked out
only the silent cones remained.

Grandson in New York City

for Andrew

Our California grandson came east with his sixth-grade class.
We had two hours to show him the Big Apple.

He said, *No thanks,* to dinosaurs at Natural History Museum,
Not really, to Chitty Chitty Bang Bang at the auto show,
but took a chance on Ground Zero at the World Trade Center
though afterhours for the 9/11 Museum.

The cascading water from the reflective pool called to him.
He stroked the stenciled names ribboned along brass borders.
His eyes reddened at a white rose caressing identical last names.

Inside the World Trade Terminal, he gazed up from marbled floor
at white elliptical ribs, and claimed to be Jonah in a whale's belly.

Outdoors, the giant Oculus
with wings outstretched, ready to soar,
lifted us.

End-of-Life Matters

My son-in-law is dying of cancer.
He tries every thing possible to hold off death.
Stoically he watches his cancer spread
from gall bladder, to liver, to lungs, to esophagus,
unstoppable by chemotherapy, radiation, and surgery.
He believes that the miracle cure is just around the bend.

However Dr. Murray's article in *The Wall Street Journal* says
terminally ill physicians die differently.
They know their choices, the limits of treatment,
and how a dying person should live.
Doctors quit their practice, spend time with their families,
write out their living wills, their advance directives,
and wait for nature to take them to that good night.

In Navajo culture, it is taboo to talk about the end of life.
They believe that negative thoughts would bring on death.
The elders want to die with dignity, like the way they lived.
When the subject of resuscitation comes up, they ask,
Why would anyone do a crazy thing like that?

Snakes and Ladders

You've worked hard when you were young
landed on the ladder of a good education
and found an easy short cut to a job
then carefully navigated through
the ups and downs of marriage,
had kids, watched them grow up,
go to college, get married and have kids of their own.

You thought you were near the top squares
and could enjoy your golden years.
You wanted to see New Zealand,
sail from Shanghai to Singapore,
attend concerts, plays, and operas in New York City.

WHAM ! You stepped into the snake's opened jaws.
Your son-in-law died of liver cancer.
Your daughter must work to support her three kids.
She called on you to help.

You saw your life spiraling down that snake
landed back to the beginning.
Must you gather courage in your old body
accept your fate to start over
and continue the game?

Part V

Unexpected Correspondence

Unexpected Correspondence

for Letty

Carefully bubble-wrapped
brown-papered and taped
it waits in my mailbox,
a message from a long-lost friend
inked on rolled birch bark.

I'm writing from the woods of Maine.
Lucy our classmate died of breast cancer.
I hear you had surgery.
Was it something, something serious?

Outside raindrops turn into snow
layering the landscape white.
Snow-burdened branches crash to earth
bringing down power lines.

In my cold, dark house I think of Maine.
In the fire-glow a woman places
stripped birch logs in the stove.

I Want to Borrow Icarus's Wings

Hurricane Sandy battered New Jersey,
flooded houses, toppled trees, blocked roads,
washed away beaches. People huddled
like cavemen in the dark.

But birds, masters of extreme weather
corrected their course when blown astray
dive-bombed like missiles for fish
used the storm as a sling shot to gain speed
and rode the gale, windsurfing through the sky.

An Unexpected Guest

As dawn was seeping through the windows
I woke from surgery and saw
my right arm hooked to an inverted bottle
my left attached to an automatic dispenser that beeped
each time it dripped morphine,
then a voice said, *Knock, knock.*

The curtains parted as an ancient monk
enveloped in a maroon cloth shuffled in.
People call me Bhante, he said.
I'm one hundred and three, where is your wound?
I pointed with my chin and mumbled,
Somewhere under the linens, I have not seen it myself.

Bhante lifted the sheet and the bloodstained gauze.
Our eyes converged on the gaping nine-inch incision
that began above the belly button
side-stepping it and continued down.
I looked away as he dropped the dressing
and pressed his heavy forearm across the lesion.

I wanted to shout, *Wait a minute.*
Someone made a mistake. I am not even a Buddhist,
but no sound came out.
The monk stood with his eyes closed as if asleep
as drops from the bottle marked time
like a water clock.

I puckered my lips and sucked in air.
I wanted to blow at his face and wake him
when Bhante opened his eyes,
announced, *You will be better,*
and staggered out, unsteady
as a prisoner in leg-irons.

The nurse came and fussed over me.
Your husband had a long visit, she said.
I wanted to laugh but the stabbing pain
reduced me to silence.

My Silence in the Hospital Room

I dreamt of being chased in the jungle.
Woke to find my pillow drenched in sweat,
plastic tubing coiled like snakes around my arms,
I feared of being swallowed by fever.

Then I saw a light
flickering like a firefly
on the lips of my roommate's silhouette.

She arrived in the early afternoon
and disappeared when the nurse said,
No food for the next twenty-four hours.
Later they found her munching
a sandwich in the cafeteria.

Tobacco smoke now gathered over me like fog.
Its outstretched hands squeezed my throat.
I wanted to scream,
Stop puffing and turn back on the air.

A glance at my shackled arms
and fear towered over me like a mounting wave.
I visualized my intravenous needles being unplugged
when I dropped off to sleep.

I decided to say nothing
and hoped when dawn waltzed in
my real or imaginary fever would dissipate
like the smoke of her cigarette.

Leaving the Adirondacks

For over thirty years many Fridays after school
our young family and the cat squeezed into the jeep
rumbled past towns and mountains, arriving
by moonlight at the cabin mirrored in a silver lake.

Enchanted by log fire, hot cider, cross-country in the snow,
hikes to garnet mines, waterfalls, mountain peaks in spring,
skinny-dipping, fireworks, watermelon on summer nights,
canoeing under canopies of flame-red leaves on fall days,
we longed to share all this with our children's children,

and never dreamt our kids would sprout wings,
fly west across the continent and stay.
Our grandchildren never came. The cat grew old and died.
The cottage, liked a jilted lover, left untouched.

Last week the realtor called.
A couple charmed by the chalet and the panorama
wanted to enjoy this enchanted place
with their sons and daughters.

We hefted boxes of books, linens, and dishes,
and left beds, canoe, skis, and firewood behind.
Red and gold leaves embraced us one last time.
We whispered *Good Luck* and drove off in the cold rain.

The Hotel with the Two-Lane Pool

After forty-seven years,
I returned to the City of Brotherly Love.
William Penn stood steadfast on top of City Hall
the Wanamaker's Organ at Macy's
trolley tracks ribboned the cobblestones
the homeless begged on Market Street.

I swam in the hotel's two-lane pool.
The rippling dance of reflective ceiling lights
on the narrow pool water mesmerized me.
I saw myself at seventeen arriving
nine-thousand-miles from home
struggling with English, Genetics, Calculus and Chemistry
unhappy with pasta, salad, and burgers in the cafeteria
unaccustomed to the noisy dormitory and the winter cold.
Only the sun and the moon looked familiar to me.
Daily I floundered in the labyrinth
until I graduated, found work, and married.
I left the city when my husband completed his degree.

Shivering, I stepped out of the twenty-five-meter lane.
Dancing light. Mirrored water. Indifferent city.

Convex/Concave

I was driving home on a cold, moonlit night
when a deer leapt out like a superhero,
impacted my right fender
and whizzed off.

I drove the car "as is" for the next four years
avoiding the five-hundred-dollar repair
until this November Sunday afternoon
by chance in the supermarket parking lot
I saw a man restore on the spot
the mangled side panel of an SUV
with a blowtorch.

For a hundred dollars he agreed to un-dent my car
instead of a blowtorch he whipped out a toilet plunger
slammed it down on the depression and pulled.
Within minutes, the Plungerman made my old car new.

Untethered

She grabs the coffee. He drags the suitcase.
Pink streaks announce sunrise at Carnegie Lake.
Few cars on the road but endless traffic lights
they ride in the silence of the long married.

Near the terminal he reminds her to water the lawn
but her eyes are glued to the carefree hawk in the sky—
concerts, lectures, and no cooking,
lull to sleep by books-on-tape at night.

As he rushes to the departure gate
jesses unfasten in her mind's eyes.
Her spirit soars to join the hawk
together they loop-de-loop the sky.

The Snake in the Wine Cup

Once on a summer solstice day in Han dynasty
Mayor Bing invited Du home. While toasting,
Du glimpsed a snake in his wine cup, but drank up.
Soon he felt ill, went home, and could not eat.

Mayor Bing sent a carriage for Du, sat him on the same seat,
poured wine and pointed to the bow mounted on the wall behind.
*What you saw in the cup was not a snake, but the shadow
of my hunting bow.* Du laughed and soon recovered.

I open my eyes, sit up and immediately fall. My world spins.
When I close my eyes, a cyclone whirlwinds my mind.
Drink more water. You're dehydrated, my husband advises.
My twirling head screams: food poison, stroke, brain tumor, MS.

Doctor says: *Your blood pressure and heartbeats are fine.*
You have benign positional vertigo.
But no worries, it can easily be fixed with exercise.
I wobble out, smile and think of the snake in Du's cup.

Wanderlust

As I goose-step on icy patches,
bundle up to shovel knee-deep snow,
my heart departs to kayak among dolphins,
seal watch at sunset on a boat,
tramp in lush green forest,
hush to hear the kiwis call,
and take cool, clear drinks from waterfalls.

I would gladly trade years
for a month of travel,
venture to somewhere new everyday,
unreachable by letters, telephones or emails.

But my life is tied to a bungee cord
that always brings me back on the rebound
no matter how far I free-fall.

The New House

I turn the key and enter—
no curtain in the shower
no chaise lounge on the patio
no television, no telephone.

Whitewashed walls—
What stories can they tell?
Were the former owners content?
How will my life unfold here?

Sitting on the hardwood floor, I watch
through naked French doors,
flashes in the darkening sky
and soon hear the drumming rain.

I step out onto wet grass.
The rain tapers.
A leaf pirouettes down
and taps me on my shoulder.

Like totems of ancestors,
the tall trees scrutinize me
curious where I come from
questioning if I belong.

Morning Ritual

Every morning I perch like a gargoyle
eyeing the pool's cold, still water
then clench my teeth and leap.

The frigid water embraces me
like tentacles of a giant octopus
I fight back with whirling arms and kicking feet.

The mantra of lap-count
and the repetition of the stroke
let my mind drift.

I try to reconstruct a line of a poem
I hear the giggling of grandkids
and think of the last dim sum with Mother.

When my hand touches the wall
for the fortieth time, I rise
and head for the hot shower.

Then step out of the gym to greet
the pink streaks of sunrise
caroling in the new day.

About the Author

Vida Chu was born in Macau and grew up in Hong Kong. She came to America to attend the University of Pennsylvania, graduated with a degree in Biology, and stayed. She has two children and four grandchildren. Her poems have appeared in many journals. A book of poems, *The Fragrant Harbor,* was published by Aldrich Press in 2014. She has children stories in *Cricket Magazine* and *"Fire and Wings,"* a children's book about dragons. She lives in Princeton, New Jersey, with her husband.

www.ingramcontent.com/pod-product-compliance
Lightning Source LLC
Chambersburg PA
CBHW031003090426
42737CB00008B/665